THE BEST FREE VERSE TEN DOLLARS CAN BUY

POEMS BY GEORGE MILLER

THE WINEBERRY PRESS   Owings, Maryland   2020

Book design by Donald Grady Shomette

Includes images by Carol Frost (p ii, 1), Lanie Shomette (p iii, 30), Carol Shomette (p 6), Lester Jay Stone (p 31).

Published in the United States of America by Wineberry Press

Manufactured in the United States of America
First Edition

Miller, George 1945— The Best Free Verse Ten Dollars Can Buy
p. cm.
Includes poems, graphics and photographs.
I. Poetry— II. Title.
Wineberry Press, Owings, MD

ISBN: 978-1-7332326-2-3.

CONTENTS

For Jenna

A CAROLINA WREN

My last memory is ashes, drifting
in a chilly breeze across her wild flowers.

Impossibly she was there while the oration droned,
while they spoke of her, she spoke to me,
her breath on my cheek, her lisp,
a whisper from the still beyond,
    Did you hear that?
  A Carolina wren.
     I taught you well.

Thereupon silence
but for the chirt of the wren.

Months later, impossibly again, my trip
homeward on the Martinsburg Express,
she slipped into the seat beside me,
whispering from her silence,
    I knew I'd find you on the early train.
  It's Friday night. Our children need me home.
    We have only a quick autumn evening,
    still and precious time,
    to be, to love.
  How, why have you returned?
    Amy, Beth, to kiss them, touch them,
    and you.
  Did my memories alone pull you back?
  or something on your side?
    Both sides are ours.

Thereupon silence,
but the wren returns each spring.

REFLECTIONS ON THE THOMAS WOLFE MEMORIAL AT THE UNIVERSITY OF NORTH CAROLINA AT CHAPEL HILL

Oh Lost and By the Wind Grieved Ghost
Come Back Again
—Thomas Wolfe, *Look Homeward Angel*

His garden graced my morning walk
along the serpentine path
through the Quadrangle.

HIs words drifted up to meet me as I passed,
a litany from his angel book, a plea to a ghost:
    Come back again.

Little did I know when I trudged across the campus,
the words etched in the stone would follow me
as I made my way through the decades.

You, my love, who share my being totally,
never again shall I know your touch, cold now,
or your song, sung so often when you lived with me.

Come, let us be together on life's serpentine path,
let us commune as angels.

BULIMIA

She approached me in the garden
where I tended inconsequential tulips.
I was busy with my auger and my bulbs
as her words drifted into earshot,
> *Dad, I need help.*
> *I drink when I should eat.*

I found her diary after she died,
the one with the embossed letters,
> *Read at your own risk.*

I opened to the final page, October 6,
the date on the page, the day in the garden,
> *2:00 PM, four hours until Bennie returns,*
> *four hours to pass without food,*
> *I can, I will.*

Clip entry after clip entry return to me in dreams,
beat on beat, a cadence, a blow to the gut.
> *2:20 PM, I flush the corn flakes down the toilet,*
> *the wedding cake saved for our anniversary,*
> *Bennie's jerky, my chocolate.*

So many friends, sisters, husband, father, mother, therapist.
how could we not sustain her? Or she herself?
> *3:02 PM, the take-out menus on the fridge,*
> *all to the dumpster, two hundred yards,*
> *three minutes there, four minutes back,*
> *time burned between the never-ending now*
> *and Bennie's hand on the door knob.*

A fateful afternoon after many near-fatal afternoons,
she jotted a ditty to pass the time,
> *3:25 PM, I have a little secret,*
> *it follows me throughout the day.*

I closed, reopened her last entry,
averted my eyes, her words remain,
strands of fine red hair drop to my lap.
> *3:55 PM, I fight the urge,*
> *vodka dulls the pain.*

Her heart stopped for lack of nurture, electrolytes,
one ten-thousandth volt to initiate a contraction,
> *4:15 PM, a walk around the block,*
> *the Greek Deli on St. Paul, I circle twice,*
> *my Dad and I eat here when he visits,*
> *I'll call him, we'll talk, he'll help.*
She didn't call.

A memory returns, our visit to Ireland,
redheaded girls on St. Stephen's Green,
> *5:02 PM, another shot of vodka,*
> *the last one helped, dulled the urge.*

Who dares say to the moment:
Stop! Enough!
> *5:45 PM, back to the dumpster for the take-out menus,*
> *I leave them on the kitchen counter beside a fifth of vodka.*

Read at your own risk, vodka dulls the pain,
a twist of lemon helps,
> *6:02 PM, Chinese carryout, $22.46,*
> *egg roll, fried rice, orange chicken,*
> *potsticker, wanton soup.*
> *I failed.*

OVERLOON

The forties after the war, the family together again,
white chocolate brownies after Thanksgiving dinner,
Momma and her sisters, cigarettes and Irish coffee,
Peggy Lee on the radio, chit-chat, smoke rings,
Granddad holds forth on Truman and Dewey,
he tamps cigar ashes onto his plate.

And I, a five year-old at the children's table,
innocent words slice through the smoke and the haze,
"Why so many aunts and so few uncles?"
Momma bolts, "Hush, Frank, be still."

And still I am till Grandma whispers:
"Your uncle Frank, you're named for him,
my son, he died in the battle at Overloon,
crushed in his tank, he's buried there,
the Dutch watch over his grave."

TWENTY MINUTE CLIFF

We met on the trails beneath the rock face,
she foraged for mushrooms in the underbrush,
I was lost, searching for the clearing
where I'd stowed my car.

She stumbled down the gully, grabbed my hand for balance,
"My name's Elsa. It's Dutch, short for Lijsbeth."

"Mushrooms," she rattled off the names:
"Hen of the woods, morels, shaggy manes."
She plucked them one by one.

"You'd best be on your way," she said.
"Twenty minutes after the sun sets
beyond the granite cliff, night, pitch black.
Let's find your car and get you out of here."

Blue eyes, alive, sparkling, a mind within, an intellect,
but mottled skin, blotches on her face and forearms.
I didn't ask. She offered when I stared.
"Too much time on the peaks above the clouds
where the sun beats down."

Years later our paths crossed again,
same trails, same mushrooms,
another lost car.

Now dark patches on her skin,
"Tumors," she explained.
"Sunlight takes its toll,
I don't have long."

Elsa knew sunset on the Blue Ridge,
twenty minutes, then pitch black.

THIRTEEN STONES

One:
An elder walks a red rock trail
to find a stone just so
to fit my palm.

He slides the stone into my hand
that I may know the land,
its touch, its feel.

Two:
A rock garden, each stone, its own,
sparse, bare, lain obliquely
to lines unseen.

No stance affords a view
into the unseen locus.

Three:
A bone-dry desert
where cacti flower.

A wasteland but for succulents
clinging to the rock face.

Four:
The red stone, her name, an unknown word,
whispered in a forgotten tongue.

Harmonics engulf the land in fifths and thirds,
wind across the rock returns her voice.

Five;
An elder scatters stones across his board,
polished crystals tumble from his leather pouch,
a mosaic, light reflected, light refracted.

Six:
Green-ringed Malachite with no other purpose
than to be her own crystalline self.

Seven:
Mercurial cinnabar,
vermilion like the flycatcher,
scarlet like the tanager.

Eight: Azurite, blue sibling of green malachite,
chromatic complement of scarlet cinnabar.

Nine:
Hessonite basks in her own rhombic splendor,
splays her voice across twelve diamond faces,
recasts light as she sees fit.

Ten:
An elder leads me to the hills that I may know
the giants who reach into the sky.

Eleven:
El Capitan, a monolith,
a bold stance above the clouds.

Twelve:
Kilauea, a molten mountain, churns below,
blows hot breath into blue island sky,
fire red rock is all he knows.

Thirteen:
Crazy Horse, Oglala Lakota,
a holy man astride his mustang,
a warrior carved into the Black Hills,
this land is his land.

THE BUCKLODGE FLAG STOP

I

A ponytail, a bandanna, a walking stick,
a chat on the knoll above the tracks,
a moment at dawn, a moment at dusk,
a quip on the gate road by the spur,
Ollie has a way to coax me with him
when we descend into his tale,
 the blizzard of '81, a grade on a curve
 in a snow storm is no place to stop a train,
 they tossed us in the snow bank
 like commandos dropped
 behind the lines.

A bandanna loft into the air, madras, gingham, paisley, plaid,
pirouettes on the platform, a dance on bricks and thistles,
flags drawn from his satchel, old-glory, lone-star, stars-and-bars,
a show for the conductor, for the dreary faces in the windows,
thumbs up, the screech of air brakes, thumbs down, the train rolls on.

The morning sun above the barns on Bucklodge Road,
the 6:22 around the bend from Barnesville,
the engineer pulls up, two coaches,
Ollie waves him on,
 too easy, the 6:22, a milk train,
 we'll wait for the big Kahuna,
 the Martinsburg express.

Rude this train screaming in the wind,
frosted eddies in December, hot dust devils in July,
we bend away before he blow us from the platform.

10 years, 2000 failed attempts before the day
we stopped the train that wouldn't stop,
Ollie's flag, the skull-and-crossbones,
his dance, the Flying Dutchman,
90 when they hit the air brakes,
Boyds when they stopped.

II

Ollie drug me to the hearing, the day they closed the flag stop,
"A menace to the public trust, we motion for a closure,"
plead the counsel for the state, "a hippie and an old fart,
let's run these trains on time."

The magistrate nodded his agreement,
"Let trains and hearings run on time."
He fumbled with his watch, then turned to Ollie,
"Who speaks for flag stops? two minutes," he decreed.

Ollie pounded on table, he strutted on the floor,
a final *Heigh-De-Ho* for Bucklodge,
a dance for those who do not dance,
the state was unimpressed.

III

Last Sunday morning as my family slept,
I drove my truck to Bucklodge and whacked
away the weeds and scrapped the soil back
from the bricks where the platform sinks
into the years and kicked aside an ice box,
abandoned, the yahoos didn't want it any more.

A shred of cloth beneath the mold and muck, a flag,
the skull-and-crossbones, a dance on bricks and thistles,
a rumble in the rail, an eddy in the air, a blast
around the bend from Barnesville, a ghost train,
the Flying Dutchman, Ollie at the throttle,
he slows and picks me up.

7

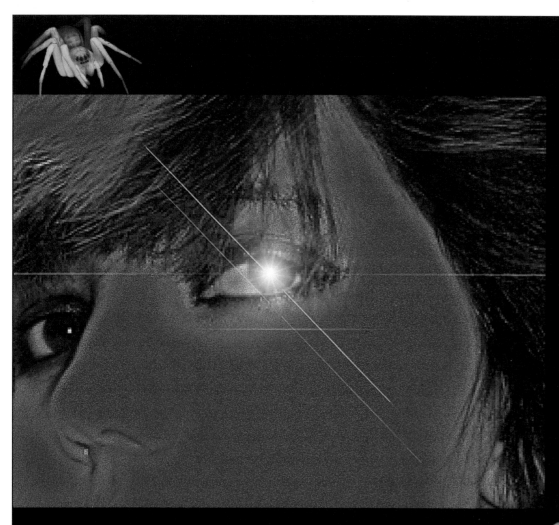

YET ANOTHER NAKED SOUL POEM

Your breath has time to straighten,
Your brain to bubble cool,
Deals one imperial thunderbolt
That scalps your naked soul.
—Emily Dickinson, *He Fumbles at Your Soul*

To be the *you* in your verse,
a second person promiscuous pronoun,
dangling as you voice your appetites.

If I can't be your *you*, let me be
a lime-green gecko toe-sucker-walking on the ceiling
as you bathe, my bulbous eyes transfixed
as you scoop chartreuse bubbles
onto freckled extremities.

If I can't be a lime-green gecko, let me be
a water spider pooter-scooting bubble-to-bubble
on the tensioned surface of your bath.

If I can't be a water spider, let me be
a free-verse poet, fantasizing
toe-sucker-walking
pooter-scooting
bulbous-eyed
naked soul.

WHAT FEELS GOOD IS GOOD

My button-down brother Larry with his soapstone hearth,
golden retriever, and lavender wisteria trellised to grow just so,
one day out of the blue proclaimed,
"What makes me feel good can't be bad."

He sprouted a handlebar mustache, spoke in nasal French,
the language of love, affairs of the heart.
    Il n'y a pas du mal à se faire du bien.

Lickety-split into the arms of his enamored coworker Michelle
for a night of intoxicated carnality lasciviously loped Larry.

"Will you get hosed?" I delicately inquired,
reminding him of pecuniary considerations,
"In retrospect might you have moved
too hastily into your demise?"

"Regrets?" he reflected in myopic hindsight
as the age-old question fluttered by the beachside gazebo
where the infidels sipped intoxicants and snorted hallucinogens,
"I regret I have but one lie to live."

"Leave no trace," I sagely advised, suspecting
a cache of undeleted messages dangling
precariously from his smartphone.

"I smell a rat," his wife Louise deduced,
following the scent from his perfumed hanky
to the cigarette butt with hot pink lipstick
carelessly discarded in the ashtray of his Peugeot.

"Perhaps an accommodation," she proposed,
considering her own mildly emotional infidelity,
a passing attraction for a poet at the coffee shop,
a charismatic gentleman with magnificent librettos.

Her secret shadow self emerged, buried long ago
beneath her split-level spouse persona,
entangled with the just so suffocating wisteria
strangulating her self-esteem,
"Neither of us ought never forego the right
to exercise our creator-endowed freewill.
Let's schedule hump day, Wednesday night,
you go your way, I'll go mine."

Larry, facing a self-made existential dilemma,
the choice between an open-minded spouse
and his lover in a split-to-the-waist blouse,
tail between his legs, limped sheepishly home.
"Perhaps I moved too hastily
for hedonism flowers most heartily
when balanced with morality."

Regrettably a mind once open is not easily closed,
come Wednesday, Louise ventured into a world
of mind-numbing freewill and heart-stopping librettos.

As the French say,
    Il n'y a pas du mal à se faire du bien.

THE ICE POND

December after the first hard freeze,
we strap our skates, glide onto the ice,
Dad, then Susan, then me, one by one,
slice into the cold.

Dad played goalie for the Lake Otters before the war,
my father the coach, his words sharp across the ice,
his booming voice delivers the hockey lecture,
the hard shaft against my palm,
    Grip the stick, David, become the stick,
    swing through the puck.

Another lecture booms across the ice,
figure skating, angular momentum,
    Pull in your arms, you'll spin faster,
    spread your arms when you want to stop,
    trust me, Susan, I'll catch you.

We three blend into the Minnesota white,
Dad's gift to us, his lakes, his winter, his world.

We skate into the December twilight,
frozen canals across barley fields,
Dad, Susan, and me,
    a lot of ponds out there, kids,
    a lot of ice.

ICE, MAST-HIGH

And now there came both mist and snow,
And it grew wondrous cold,
And ice, mast-high, came floating by.
— Samuel Taylor Coleridge, *The Rime of the Ancient Mariner*

Autumn, the Year 925, End of the First Millennium.

A boat on the North Sea: one man, two wives, three daughters,
six sons, eight loaves, two sheep, one raven.

Weeks on the waters, alone among rogue waves,
leagues beyond Norway, leagues short of Iceland.

A Norseman tacks windward into the gale,
lost but for ...
... he stands on the bow,
        opens the cage,
                prays to Lord Odin,
                        releases the raven.

They follow the bird to the Shetland shore.

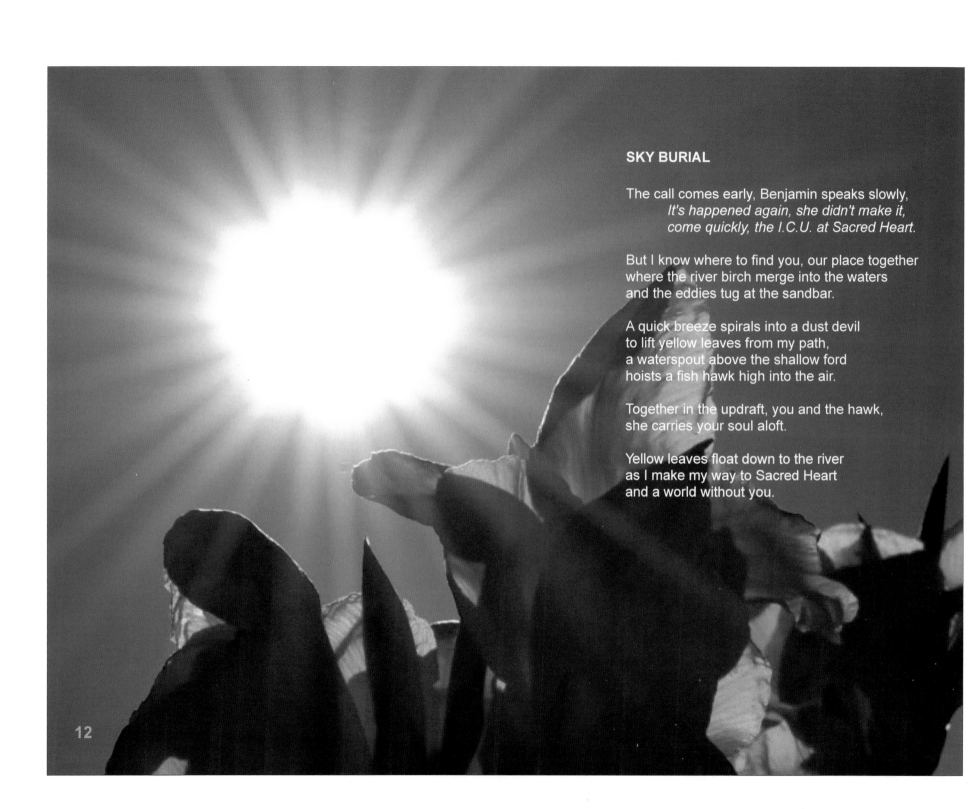

SKY BURIAL

The call comes early, Benjamin speaks slowly,
It's happened again, she didn't make it,
come quickly, the I.C.U. at Sacred Heart.

But I know where to find you, our place together
where the river birch merge into the waters
and the eddies tug at the sandbar.

A quick breeze spirals into a dust devil
to lift yellow leaves from my path,
a waterspout above the shallow ford
hoists a fish hawk high into the air.

Together in the updraft, you and the hawk,
she carries your soul aloft.

Yellow leaves float down to the river
as I make my way to Sacred Heart
and a world without you.

EASTER - ST. MARY'S COUNTY - MARYLAND - 1817

We know their dream; enough
To know they dreamed and are dead;
   —WB Yeats, *Easter 1916*

Dawn on resurrection day, the fields of St. Inigoes,
be there, close your eyes, listen for the voices,
hear the rocks and clubs pelt against the storefront,
feel the uprising in your bones, the rage.

Doomed to fall short, free for a few brief hours,
slaves battled through the half-light.

Insurrection, a crime against the state,
against men who owned men,
men who owned the narrative.

Dog packs, blood hounds, tracked human scent
into the marsh, property became prey.

Through whose eyes do we view ignominy?
Masters whose sleight of hand shuffled memories
deep into history's deck?

Recollections faded bit by bit, layer on layer
as landlocked tobacco ports succumbed to silt
flushed from the fields where they endured.

Come, lay a wreath on Easter sunrise,
sanctify the ground where they were chained,
dispatched to Louisiana's stifling cotton fields,
whipped, brutalized, sold.

The fields of St. Inigoes, little has changed
where men sought the terribly beautiful hours
of a free dawn.

"One hour before sunset on Easter Monday 1817 over 150 slaves and free blacks gathered at St. Inigoes store and were accused of attempted insurrection," Nancy Radcliffe, then a St. Mary's College student, wrote in a research paper that drew much of its description of the event from an article in the New York Evening Post on April 21, 1817. http://www.somd*news.com/enterprise/spotlight/those-enslaved-in-southern-mayland-* resisted/article_

14

SATURDAY AFTERNOON ON PATTERSON AVENUE

Joseph sits at the table, leafs through the paper, puffs on his pipe,
   My sister was the most beautiful woman. Her hair was fiery red.

Ruth pulls her sweater up to her chin.
   Papa made nice fires. He kept us warm.

Joseph drops the newspaper to the floor.
   My sister made wonderful goat cheese.
   It was firm, not like the goat cheese in the stores.

Ruth spreads cucumbers onto her cutting board,
mixes spices in the palm of her hand,
sprinkles capers into sweet pickle brine.
   Papa died on a cold November morning,
   on the eleventh day of a batch of fourteen-day pickles.

Joseph stands and stretches, warming himself before the fire.
   I definitely have a yen for some goat cheese.
   You'll have to make us some goat cheese.

Ruth keeps fifty-eight-year-old eleventh-day pickles
in a glass jar in the pantry lest they too be lost.

A STOPOVER IN CLEVELAND

A visit for the weekend, Dick and Mary, passing through
on their trek across the country, Boston to San Jose,
dinner for three at my bungalow in Shaker Heights,
you'd be the fourth.

Dick finds the moment rich,
    Let's meet more often,
    life is short.

Your portrait on the wall above us,
a woolen scarf around your neck,
the plaid we bought in Edinburgh
before our trek into the highlands.

Dick's words hang before us,
the conversation stalls,
    Short indeed.

Mary sweeps the words aside,
she takes my hand.
    How long's it been?
    Seems like yesterday
    when she was here.

You wore the scarf when you slipped away,
three years it's been, like yesterday.

Lifelong friends, red wine, roasted scallops,
another day, another meal without you.

REVERBERATIONS FROM A LIMESTONE CLIFF - CUBA - 2017

Our day begins long before we glide into the parking lot,
a gravy biscuit breakfast, a flat tire on rutted gravel roads,
a steep slope snaking off the plateau into the woodlands.

Girardo lifts the microphone to his lips, eases into English,
our bus descends to the wetland forest.
> *Today our target bird, the Cuban Solitaire,*
> *a nightingale, number 13 of our 22 endemics,*
> *we'll hear his song against the limestone cliff.*
> *you'll find this glen enthralling,*
> *a bit of song, a bit of lore.*

He leads the way into the thicket, we trail behind,
himself a Cuban endemic, native to the island, nowhere else,
he pivots the scope from his shoulder, a tight quick move,
his practiced aim brings the bird to focus,
> *Have a look, there above the horizontal branch,*
> *dingy brown but what a song.*

He scans the cliff to catch harmonics off the limestone,
ears cocked, deft footwork to find the sweet spot,
> *Gather round me here*
> *where the sounds converge,*
> *resonant to your core.*

An acoustic lesson, Spanish inflection atop clipped English,
we crowd into the vortex to listen,
> *Limestone reflects the high-pitched call,*
> *absorbs the low rustling background.*

The bird song fades, again he cups his hands behind his ears,
scans the parabolic cliff, silence as he listens,
we follow to a cave beneath the bromeliad,
> *Voices percolate from the rock,*
> *ancient springs seep through the walls,*
> *a time capsule.*

Again we gather tightly together,
he brings the decades to life,
the past rises before us,
> *Here Che Guevara bivouacked the western army,*
> *a place to hide while the world stoked missiles,*
> *close your eyes, you see him at his chessboard,*
> *you feel the revolution in your bones.*

Girardo slips his hands into his blue jean pockets,
birdsong gives way to chit-chat, one by one we amble back,
the bus snakes up the rutted road, he lifts the microphone,
> *This afternoon our target, the Bee Hummingbird,*
> *number 14 of our 22 endemics, the world's smallest bird.*

BOOT-CUT JEANS

We share each other's jeans, my mother and I, size 8 on a good day,
Hudson Signature Boot-cuts, my mother shops at Nordstroms.

I snag a pair from the laundry hamper on my morning dash to meet the bus,
I plumb the pocket for the fare, for dimes and quarters, I find a note,
> *I see you're in the city Tuesday,*
> *the planning council at the church pavilion,*
> *lunch at half-past twelve,*
> *the deli on the wharf.*

The school bus pulls up, the driver toots his horn, I wave him on,
my classmates in the windows jeer at me
crying at the bus stop on Tanners Row.
I'll not be in school today.

I read his note again, his slow seductive cursive,
plumb jaunts for I's and L's, plump round O's and A's,
quick strokes through F's and T's, a piercing hand,
he loads the words into the breach,
> *Then maybe if we're lucky,*
> *my apartment on St. Paul,*
> *it's been too long,*
> *the church can wait.*

I've seen the envelope before, the letterhead, All Souls All Saints,
I know the place to look, the alcove in the attic, Grandma's rosewood vanity,
a cigar box tucked beneath the linen, my mother's keepsakes neatly bound in twine,
I tug, the knot gives way, their letters spill into my hand.

All these years with Mom and Dad, we read together on my bed,
cotton sheets with stars and moons, so cozy, so false,
Little Women, Meg, Jo, Beth, and Amy, a fairytale,
> *Is everything a lie?*

My mother takes her mornings slow, yoga in the den,
the Times and coffee on the couch, she's fortified for all
except a fury storming down the stairs,
> *Cotton sheets with stars and moons, my ass!*

All Souls All Saints, the Church on North Charles where he ministers his flock,
his apartment on St. Paul where he steals my mother's love,
one by one, blow by blow, I slam his letters on her desk,
> *Mom, I have to know.*

FREDERICKSBURG BATTLEFIELD - 2019

What stays with you latest and deepest?
—Walt Whitman, *Drum Taps*

Questions as I retrace your footsteps into the heights,
yours and your compatriots', Pennsylvania Volunteers,
farmers become riflemen, teachers become cannoneers,
an ill-conceived march into the breach
that never opened.

You, my father's father's father, my flesh, my blood,
did you lie injured on the field through the night?
Was your voice among the wailing wounded?

Could you not, as I cannot, comprehend
the catastrophe?

A question from the boy we both once were:
"The arm you lost, where is it?
Did you feel a phantom tingle
when you plowed your field?"

My girlfriend trudges along beside me
while I wander the stone wall, the sunken road,
she grabs my arm, her face in mine,
a question explodes within her gut, splatters:
"What did his mother feel? she who lost
two children to whooping cough, one in childbirth,
his brother to the war, her husband to consumption?
Did she curse the insanity?"

Are you alive within me, in that place where I brood?
Is my melancholy yours for your lost companions?
Is my grief your mother's for her lost children?

Your comrades, did they find their way home as you did?
The others who did not, did you visit their graves?

My girlfriend again, an angry voice, a question on the heights
where Generals Lee and Longstreet surveyed the slaughter:
"Do men ever learn anything? Did you ever consider,
the world would be better off run by women?"

A question for the wound dresser, the bearded poet,
who searched the hospital tents for his fallen brother:
When you saw *the stretchers lying ... untended lying,*
did you happen upon my great-grandfather,
William Boston Miller, the teacher, the farmer,
wounded, bleeding?

What stays with me? The bearded poet
who sings for all, who sang for you,
we read his lilac elegy and mourn.

A question for the surgeon:
When you sawed off arms and legs,
did you happen upon his hand? a wedding ring?
inscribed, gold script*: With love, your Katie,*
we want it back.

THE CROSSING

I

The farmhouse was Toni's dream: trumpet vines on the trellis,
a porch and a swing on the palisade above the North Branch,
lavender trim on periwinkle clapboard, a rose-hip door.

Breakfast as the day began: goat cheese on Jewish rye,
coffee on the deck where she sketched the ridge line on her pad,
Haystack Mountain and the Algonquin Heights.

II

Post oaks on the gate road over the bluff onto the bottom,
a rutted lane submerged by sandy eddies at the ford,
the North Branch broad around the bend,
tire tracks at the water's edge.

A kingfisher in the river birch above the crossing,
a hollow rattle, *lie here, lie cold, lie dead, lie still.*

A bitter slog against the wind, I wade across the ford,
an icy visit to the graveyard on the other side.

III

Sunday afternoon, a visit from my sister Claire,
she whispers as she takes my hand, she means no harm:
this place could use a coat of paint.

The periwinkle and the rose-hip fade,
the dream plods on without the dreamer.

19

THE REAR EXIT

The rear exit where I slip into the alley
among dumpsters and yellow street lamps,
where your voice echos, "Daddy, stay with me."

The hospital where I held your hand for the last time,
where scopes traced your heart's feeble beat,
where the wind that cannot be
eased into the place that isn't.

One by one, alarms paged nurses and doctors,
blue scrubs burst through the door as you slipped away,
then one by one retreated to the safety of their stations
to record your passing in their charts.

The long vigil through the dark night, over,
I lifted my head to a world dawning without you.

The rear exit where I slip into the alley
among dumpsters and yellow street lamps,
where your voice echos.

THE LOFT

My mother calls me to her loft, her place apart,
the nook above the boathouse, her own, beyond,
she sets her work aside,
> *So good of you to come,*
> *just a little chat before the day begins,*
> *that's all.*

She knows I know, she stands, she never stands,
she folds her glasses, cups them in her hand,
too close, her hands, her words,
I have to get away,
> *Your father loves you as I do,*
> *the love we share,*
> *you'll see us both,*
> *of course.*

She draws me to her side, she barely moves her lips,
her slow tidewater Virginian drawl,
her voice I love, her words I hate,
> *Another place, another time, another man,*
> *I fell in love, there's little more to say,*
> *lunches on the wharf, drinks after work,*
> *weekends on the river, sunsets on the marsh.*
> *too easily together, too often,*
> *we meant no harm, none.*

My mother drifts from then-and-there to here-and-now
as if she speaks of little else than laundry in the hamper.

CAMPAIGN RIBBON

An easy chair, an olive drab footlocker,
a table and a lamp, a hutch in the attic,
I hunker down, I nurse a glass of scotch,
neat from an amber bottle.

A campaign ribbon, six points, a green disk, a gold star,
a white star, gherkin green and pale white stripes,
three red ray flames consume a splintered country.

A deadly sweep through the valley,
a tainted battalion, I didn't know
when I brought the ribbon home
about the long cruel decades,
the scotch.

THREE GRACES AND THEIR HOUSES

Grace Carleton speaks with a lisp,
Grace Farley hides behind a poker face,
Grace Marlow talks hardly at all.

Carly built her cabin in the old growth cedar,
heartwood chiseled from trees she felled,
brawn, sweat, will, grit, layered
log on log, notched and hewn.

She guards her woodland from her porch,
shotgun in her lap, bulldogs at her feet,
sentries to ward off eavesdroppers
within earshot of her lisp.

Farley chose a loft in the heart of the town,
her abode atop an ancient barley mill,
she wanders her rooftop with a Nikon lens,
frames her shots into the streets below,
dancers, hucksters, falcons, dumpsters,
paupers, strollers, hipsters, smokers, drunks.

Photos shroud her walls, floor to ceiling,
her fervent vision unfolds before my eyes
when I gaze upon her distal shots
into the wild, the tame,
the lame, the insane.

Marly when she speaks, she sings,
lyrics plucked on silk-wound strings,
harmonics beyond belief,
perfect fifths.

She chose the bungalow at First and Main,
rocker on her porch, mandolin in her lap,
elms in her yard, cats at her feet,
she masks balladic words
behind a veil of verse.

Carly layered the logs,
Farley bared our stories,
Marly shared her song,
I tagged along.

23

ONCE MORE INTO THE BREACH

3:00 AM — a dark room, Falstaff rocks side to side,
front paws kneading the cotton cord of the throw rug,
tail twitching methodically through stale bedroom air
lockstep with mental machinations behind feline eyes.

Tail position, thrust vector, distance, throw weight,
so many considerations for each and every destination,
dresser, chandelier, bed board, armoire.

A silent countdown within, a transformation without,
roly-poly barn cat morphs to long, lean leaper,
his steely eyes lock onto the bed board,
his tail snaps, releasing his cocked body.

Henry dreams deliciously, deviled crabs and sweet potato fries,
a peaceful sleep on four-poster memory-foam.

Peaceful but for the swoosh of the throw rug across the hard-waxed floor,
the clatter and gurgle of empty and half-empty beer cans
as they're scattered like tenpins before the rug.

Peaceful but for the tormented squeal of Falstaff hanging from the bed board,
his claws tangled in the frayed threads of Henry's bird of paradise quilt.

Rising from disheveled sheets, struggling to the conscious surface,
fingers groping through the shadows for his imperiled cat,
Henry separates paw and quilt, nail by nail, thread by thread.

5:00 AM — Henry dreams again, Czech sausage, pilsner, and sauerkraut,
Falstaff lies tranquilly at his side, purrs as Henry snoozes.

EXCALIBUR

If you can pull a poem from your ass
when others struggle with their constipated blocks

If you can pull a poem from your ass
when hecklers fling spit wads at your open mic,
saliva soaked projectiles splatter on your forehead

If you can pull a poem from your ass
when pedants belittle your amateur sketches,
 your goats, riverboats, peat bog fires,
 deceased lovers, labor day pig roasts

If you can pull a poem from your ass
when you sell hip-pity-hop jingles to marketeers,
your lines chime like soap commercials

If you can pull a poem from your ass
when the caption bubble in your cartoon life deflates,
the funny paper light bulb floating above your head
dims as you run out of ideas

If you can pull a poem from your ass,
etch a few heartfelt lines on the unforgiving stone,
script a few words for the ones you love, dead or alive

If you can pull a poem from your ass,
couplets to skim the surface like water spiders,
to nest among the duckweed and the cinnamon fern

If you can pull a poem from your ass,
then your words will find their way,
a pleasant journey,
trust me.

A Devocion del R Padre
Fidel Gasbillo y familia
Copacabana. 27 de Junio 1946

26

STATIONS OF THE CROSS

My therapist sits across the coffee table, lifts a book to her lap,
"Do you know the poet Louise Gluck?" she asks as she reads.
> *I was, you will understand, entering the kingdom of death.*
> *As we had all been flesh together, now we were mist.*
> —Louise Gluck, *Faithful and Virtuous Night*

She leans back and folds her arms,
draws herself cross-legged up into her chair,
"Let's talk about your dream."

You, my child, who wander the nocturnal passage,
formless but for your voice, you cry as you pass,
station by station, through the etched stone crosses.

You, the infant, who tumbled from your mother's womb into my arms,
I didn't know your form until I held you, a baby girl,
red hair, pale skin, blue eyes, soft voice.

You, the toddler, who bounced on my shoulders,
who lived in my house, the alcove in the attic,
daily we sat at the breakfast table.

What of you when I no longer weave the fabrics,
when there's no kindred incarnation to sustain you,
when I no longer dream?

Together we ascend the path winding up the mountain,
we make our way onto the pale landscape above the horizons
where only stars delineate our passage.

You, a shadow, trail behind me
as we trudge along the rocky path,
station by station, father and daughter,
lockstep.

BIG SISTER

Friday afternoon, Anna home again,
pale on the swing, Mom at her side,
hand in hand.

Dad in the rocker, gatekeeper of *do's* and *don't's,*
cautions as he reads the doctors' notes:
    Speak one at a time and slowly.
    Not too much to stimulate the senses.
    She'll not process as nimbly as before.
He drops the paper to his knee, folds his glasses:
    Tomorrow perhaps a visit to the market,
    but let the sun set gently on today.

Sally, Hank and me, siblings on the steps,
we speak when Dad cues, slowly,
one at a time from a distance,
soft words to kindle memory.
    So nice to have you home again,
    Tomorrow perhaps a walk into the woods.
    You like it there along the stream.

Home, day one without a seizure,
Anna on the porch swing,
    Yes, a walk into the woods, nice.

RED GARLAND AT THE ONE STEP DOWN
PENNSYLVANIA AVENUE, SEPTEMBER 21, 1974

A wah-wah mute on a B-flat coronet,
aluminum on cork on brass,
three fingers on three valves.

Four-finger chords on ivory keys,
inversions, his right hand follows his left.

A melody plucked from cat gut strings,
  Where have you been, Billy Boy?

Wire brushes on taut leather drumhead,
measure after staggered measure,
  I've been to seek a wife.

They lead, they follow, they wander,
Billy Boy with a Cha-Cha-Cha,
  There's a dimple on her chin.

Unborn sixteenth notes
of a wildly syncopated tune
wander to a distal realm,
  She's a young thing.

Block chords, four-finger rhythm,
three-finger melody, bounce, tease,
  She can sing a pretty song,
  but she often sings it wrong.

Wah-Wah, Cha-Cha,
  She cannot leave her mother.

THINGS MY GOAT ATE

Momma's black satin choir robe,
Brother Oliver's olive drab canvas rucksack,
Cousin Pattie's patent leather penny loafers,
Uncle Paul's double wide purple paisley necktie,
Grandpa Charlie's chief petty officer warm weather tunic,
Aunt Gretchen's *Mother Jones* April 1993 sex and power edition,
My gherkin green and pale white striped Vietnam campaign ribbon,
Brother-in-law Vennie's vinyl 45 RPM *Ballad of Thunder Road,*
Sister Kate's signed first edition *Reflections in a Golden Eye,*
Daddy's fire engine red Bill Grogan railroad shirt,
Grandma Cherry's butterfly and herb garden
down to the nubby gnarly roots.

29

**CONVERSATION
ON THE WAY
TO THE
ELEMENTARY
SCHOOL**

(daughter) Did Momma have any boyfriends before you?
(me) There was one boy, Joe, in high school.
(daughter) Was he nice?
(me) No, he was a football player.
(daughter) Did she love him?
(me) It was a long time ago and it was high school.
(daughter) Do people love each other in high school?
(me) Not very well.
(daughter) But later they do?
(me) Maybe a little better.
(daughter) Momma says you are a good man and she met you in college.
(me) Your momma is a smart woman.
(daughter) Where is Joe now? Is he married?
(me) He's not with us any more. Unfortunately he died.
(daughter) But you said he was in high school.
(me) He was and then he wasn't and then he was dead.
(daughter) How did he die?
(me) It was a car accident.
(daughter) Was he drunk? Momma says you should never drink and drive.
(me) Your momma is a smart woman.
(daughter) Was Joe drunk?
(me) Yes, he was.
(daughter) Did Momma love him after he was dead?
(me) For a little while but that was high school.
(daughter) Was Momma crying about Joe last night?
(me) Sometimes she worries she'll lose us the way she lost Joe.
(daughter) Can you love someone after they are dead? Is there an angel that you love?
(me) Sometimes we love the memories and sometimes maybe there is an angel.

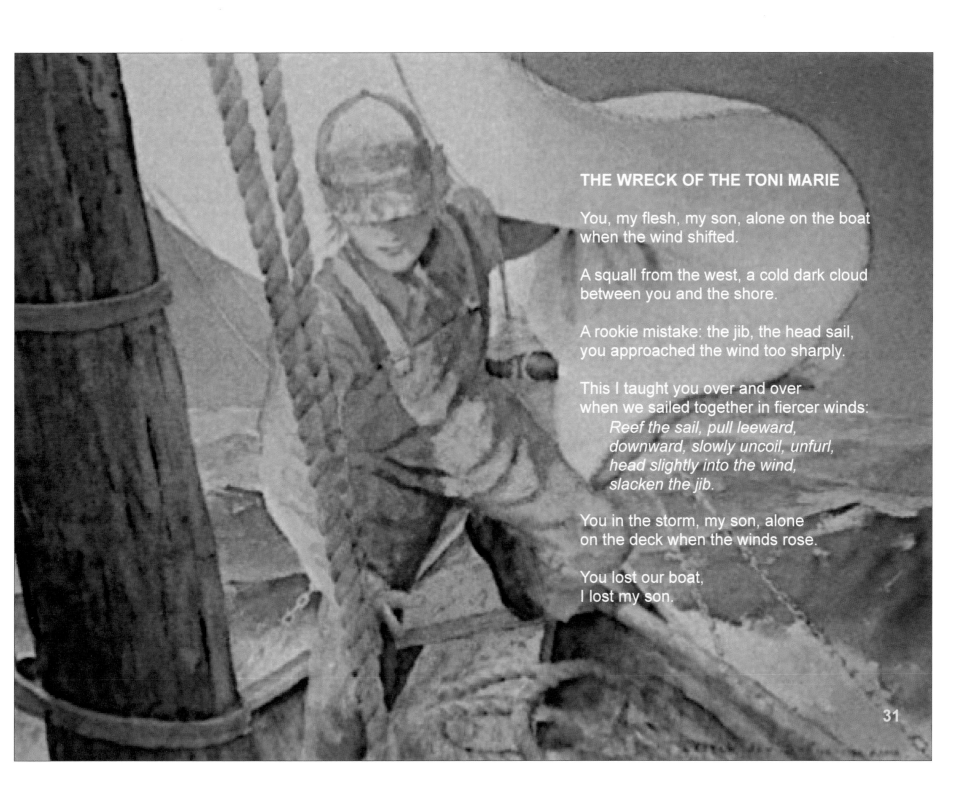

THE WRECK OF THE TONI MARIE

You, my flesh, my son, alone on the boat
when the wind shifted.

A squall from the west, a cold dark cloud
between you and the shore.

A rookie mistake: the jib, the head sail,
you approached the wind too sharply.

This I taught you over and over
when we sailed together in fiercer winds:
> Reef the sail, pull leeward,
> downward, slowly uncoil, unfurl,
> head slightly into the wind,
> slacken the jib.

You in the storm, my son, alone
on the deck when the winds rose.

You lost our boat,
I lost my son.

31

LOST IN TRANSMIGRATION

I

A peanut shell, face-down among the beer cans,
corn cobs, and chicken bones of the Labor Day pig roast.

A chipmunk nibbles on the shell, a rat snake slithers
through the grass, a barn owl circles, poised
for the exact moment between dusk and dark
when the rat snake slows in the cool evening.

A peanut shell, a brief incarnation before it disappears
into a chipmunk belly and then into a rat snake belly
and then into a barn owl belly.

A peanut soul, soon to be transmigrated within a chipmunk soul
and then within a rat snake soul and then within a barn owl soul.

II

My drunken brother dropped his plate on his way to take a pee
in the bushes after a night of intoxication
at the Labor Day pig roast.

I fear for his soul, face-down among the corn cobs and chicken bones,
among tiny flecks of peanut, chipmunk, rat snake, and barn owl.

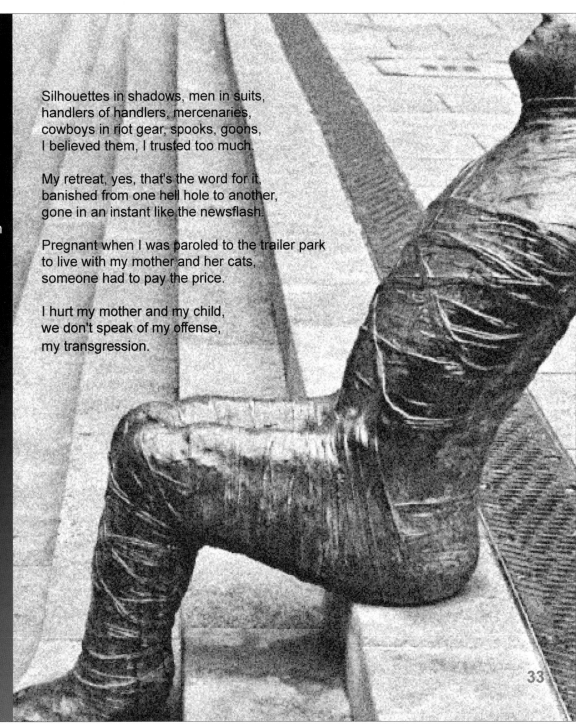

POSTER CHILD

Dogs on leases, naked Hadji on hands and knees,
sand storms blow across the hot dry desert
into the prison yard where we stand guard
over the bushy bearded boys.

The evening news preceded my retreat, a bolt,
satellite to satellite, earth to sky, electric, hot,
an instant from the press room in Baghdad
to an antenna dish on a double wide in Cresaptown
where my mother and my aunt lunched
over grilled cheese at the kitchen table.

"That can't be Sophie, can it?"
"Surely not, I raised her better."

The proposition seemed simple once, so easy,
a recruiter, the army reserve, a sweet contract,
two hundred bucks for a weekend once a month,
tuition as I worked my way from grocery clerk
to classes at the junior college.

Then my unit deployed, lawyers, mechanics,
grocery clerks, students, mothers with babies,
one day Cumberland for high school football,
the next the hell hole, the prison Abu Ghraib.

Silhouettes in shadows, men in suits,
handlers of handlers, mercenaries,
cowboys in riot gear, spooks, goons,
I believed them, I trusted too much.

My retreat, yes, that's the word for it,
banished from one hell hole to another,
gone in an instant like the newsflash.

Pregnant when I was paroled to the trailer park
to live with my mother and her cats,
someone had to pay the price.

I hurt my mother and my child,
we don't speak of my offense,
my transgression.

Baltimore Sun, APR 30, 2004, 3:00 AM: Just days ago,
the Army's 372nd Military Police Company, based near
Cumberland, was the source of unabashed pride in the city. That
changed Wednesday when the country found out that members
of the unit, deployed in Iraq, have been accused of committing
crimes against Iraqi prisoners.

33

BURIAL AT TANNERS ROW

Grandma took her morning constitutional on the causeway into town,
Tanners Row to French Creek, a mile and a half with a walking cane,
high-water pants, strawberry prints, day-glow flip-flops,
prune juice and bran flakes at the French Creek Diner.

I carried her bag and her web-weave chair for stops along the way,
a smoke with the crabbers on the sandbar, she called them by their names,
Not bad for a dip net and hand line, Betty,
leave some for the rest of us, Jamar.

When I was eight, a morning oath beneath the French Creek drawbridge,
Grandma and Helen, age spots and freckles,
we pinky swear, pals till the end.

Grandma died when I was ten; we buried her at Tanners Row,
her home and ours, a simple service for a wayward soul;
the Rector whispered from his book of prayer,
May her soul through the mercy of God rest in peace.

My father gave the nod; the undertaker turned the crank;
Grandma dropped into her grave on the willow knoll atop the bluff.

My mother chatted up the guests who'd come to say goodbye;
she hit the high notes on the landing by the boathouse,
And let's not forget, Grandma on the infield at the Preakness,
in her Karmann Ghia on the road to Chincoteague,
at the Harbor for the Tall Ships.

Her voice dropped to contralto, the octave where she conjured selves and shadows,
farewell to Grandma on the garden bench where we sat to watch the sunset;
So many mornings at the window in my office loft,
I swiveled in my chair to catch the river view,
you and Grandma on the causeway,
I never took the time to tag along.

34

DENISE'S SECOND COMING

Grave robbers have snatched Denise.
For years I kept her ashes in a whiskey bottle
in the back of the liquor cabinet.

Then last October
I almost drank her for a nightcap;
so I hid her in an oatmeal box in the pantry.

Yesterday morning my drunken brother Arnold
and his slut of a girlfriend Susan ate her for breakfast.

JANET LYNN HOFBERGER

Hers was a long-legged stride, her grandmother's stubborn stride
across Mechanic Street past the post office to the dairy.

A black burlap handbag slung over her shoulder, her arm clamped over the flap,
she paused in the sun as she dug through her bag for her lip balm.

"Hey, college boy! Get a job!" her words rattled up the block to the tire outlet
where my brother Jennings and I waited for our father's mechanic
to fit the Thunderbird with snow tires.

"Hey! Where'd you learn to park?" I shot back,
her pale green Packard spanned two slots
in the side lot of the train depot.

She squared her stance across the road,
"I do the best I can with that the good lord gave me."

Jennings whispered under his breath,
"The good lord was awfully generous."
He leaned closer with our own grandmother's twinkle in his eye,
"She wants you, yes, I believe she does."

"Hey, college boy! Is your daddy paying for those tires?"
Janet fired a final salvo before she disappeared into the dairy.

One day long ago on the Friday after Thanksgiving,
Janet Lynn Hofberger waltzed along Mechanic Street
with an invitation in her eye and I allowed the moment to pass.

The hour is late, the vigil strays into another day,
Sacred Heart, the hospice on the hill above the town,
Jennings lounges in the chair beside my bed,
he takes my hand, I share my final thought,
"Our daddy paid for those tires."

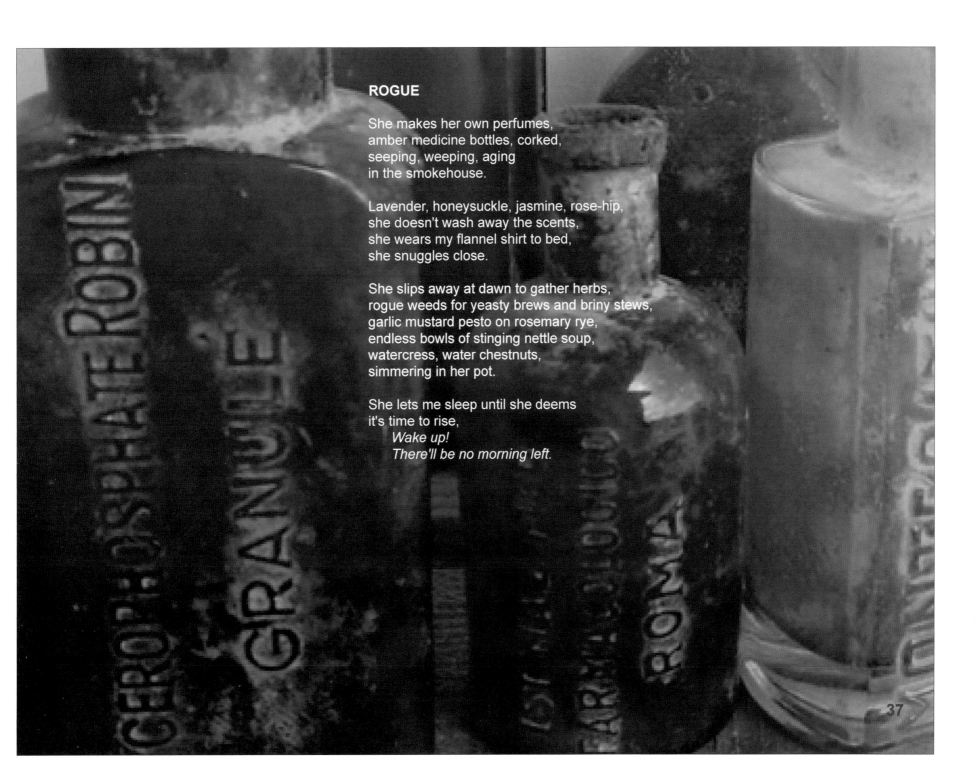

ROGUE

She makes her own perfumes,
amber medicine bottles, corked,
seeping, weeping, aging
in the smokehouse.

Lavender, honeysuckle, jasmine, rose-hip,
she doesn't wash away the scents,
she wears my flannel shirt to bed,
she snuggles close.

She slips away at dawn to gather herbs,
rogue weeds for yeasty brews and briny stews,
garlic mustard pesto on rosemary rye,
endless bowls of stinging nettle soup,
watercress, water chestnuts,
simmering in her pot.

She lets me sleep until she deems
it's time to rise,
    Wake up!
    There'll be no morning left.

THE ROYAL BOTANIC GARDENS - SYDNEY - 2017

Our day began before the sun rose to its midday swelter,
hours before the swollen ankles, blisters, grumbling,
we wandered serpentine paths among the eucalyptus,
marveled at blue fairy wren foraging in the red sage,
white-cheeked honeyeaters nesting in the firewood.

As the afternoon wore on, as the magic ebbed,
our conversation digressed,
> *this must be the way.*
>> *no, there, church spires in the distance,*
>> *Potts Point and our hotel.*
> *no, the path beyond the hill crest*
> *skirts the slope, there we'll find the light rail.*
>> *I've only so much left in me,*
>> *let's not waste it on your hunches.*

Carol spotted him first, his bus parked beneath the blue gum,
he, South Asian, an Indian, we, American tourists, sunburned,
> *can you get us out of here,*
> *Potts Point and our hotel?*

We approached, he crushed his cigarette beneath his shoe,
climbed into the driver's seat behind the plexiglass,
> *that's not my route, but I'll take you to Central Rail*
> *for a transfer to Kings Cross.*

We took our seats, Carol asked,
> *what did you think of our election?*
He swiveled to face us, scoped us out before he spoke,
> *depends which side of the coin you're on.*

Then he unloaded, words erupting through the sticky afternoon,
> *the man is a capitalist, pure and simple,*
> *but there is no price on compassion, family, hope,*
> *he doesn't see beyond the darkened windows*
> *of his limousine nosing through the crowds.*

Done, a schedule to keep, he swiveled back to face his route,
the bus eased forward, skirting the gardens into Sydney.

Yet today we envy the language and culture of a stranger
whose crisply spoken diatribe bares feelings we failed to articulate.

POOCH

My exwife's exhusband's exwife's ex
left her left him left her left me
thirteen dogs: Abigail, Swede, Walter,
Poor Richard, Freddie, Rodin, Sister,
Delta Queen, Alice B, Schwarz, Rollback,
Suwannee, and Light Horse Harry Lee.

The ex's ex's ex's ex lives in anguish,
the ex's ex's ex in emotional retreat,
the ex's ex with my record collection,
the ex with the ex's ex's staph infection.

Still and all, my dogs greet me at the end
of the day with brown eyes eager
for a romp in the park. I could be a happy man
if the ex's ex returned my records,
but, hey, you can't have everything.

A DAY AT THE OFFICE OF MANAGEMENT AND BUDGET

Budget season when the wonks and gnomes gather
at 17th and Pennsylvania to fabricate the ledgers,
to collate vast trillions into columns and rows
on hard black binders.

One September morning long days into the grand prevarication,
Agnes Worthington snapped, refused to force-balance
gherkin green and pale white lines on her accounts.
"I've had it with numbers, there's got to be more."

Her mother didn't raise her to skim pennies from coffers
of widows and orphans or fudge the cost of war.

"One step at a time, let's work this through,"
cajoled her mates from the desks on the floor,
but snapped was snapped, her spring had sprung,
what could we do with her numbers askew?

Suggestions abounded from geeks on the servers,
think-tankers pontificating high in the loft,
number-crunchers on cubicle row.
>   *perhaps some air,*
>   *a walk in the park,*
>   *dark chocolate,*
>   *oatmeal with flaxseed,*
>   *a nip at the tavern,*
>   *shopping, always the cure*
>   *whatever the cause.*

"Yes, a stroll through the park," the crunchers concurred,
"One of our own has crashed."

Hand upon hand we agreed, Lafayette Square for lunch,
moussaka, gyros, half-smokes from the Lebanese deli,
bocce on the grass with tourists from Kansas,
a cure beyond shopping and flaxseed,
our freckled bespeckled macroeconomist
let down her strawberry blond ballerina bun,
a smirk on her lip, she cast off the shackles,
Agnes of Cartwheels in Lafayette Square.

The afternoon receded as one by one we trickled
back to the office for our end-of-day briefing,
duty, dollars, mouths-to-feed drew us back
to the battleship gray conference room,
budgets, black binders, ledgers, lies.

Alone on the square below, unreconstructed, undaunted,
Agnes, knee-deep in the fountain toe-diving for pennies.

(she, girlfriend) salmon? how much do we need?

(me) I said I'd take care of it.

(me the next week to the therapist) okay, here's the problem, we're in Trader Joes, there's a pot luck, we need salmon.

(she, therapist) let's get in touch with this, how have you discussed the matter?

(she, girlfriend) we're here, the salmon's here, what's to decide?

(me) I have a feel for these things, I spent a summer in Alaska, I know my salmon.

(she, therapist) did you say what you thought? expression, we've discussed that.

(she, girlfriend) let's do the math, four couples, let's say three ounces apiece, times eight, that's twenty-four ounces.

(me to the therapist) then maybe I said something like, "It's my party, I think I can handle the salmon."

(she -- I forget which one) there's a problem here, let's zero in on it.

(she, therapist) I'm not sure I follow you, what were the exact words?

(me) I think I know how to buy salmon, this is too much.

(she, therapist) that's good, assert yourself, I like it, expression, raw feelings, the inside.

(she, girlfriend) twenty-four ounces is about right, any more and people fill up before the main course, we're talking appetizer here.

(she, therapist) I can't believe I'm taking the man's side on this.

(she, girlfriend) okay, that's two twelve-ounce packages.

(she, therapist) I hate to interrupt here but we're out of time.

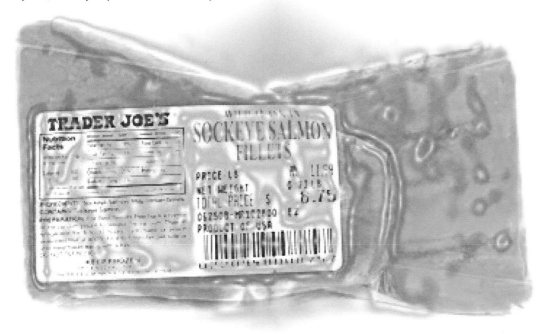

An opera on the boom-box, a slow Saturday brunch
in the sun room, a simple feast, poached eggs on rye,
a fine season on South Mountain.

Henry ,the maestro with the butter-knife-baton,
yodels along with the compact disc
in his lean, low baritone:
How about a few extra rows of corn or scallions
or snaps or squash or turnips in the spring?
and Denise (what a pair of lungs on that woman)
in an earthy contralto rejoins:
I am all for more veggies but please
no more turnips. I have had my fill for a lifetime.

42

Long legs and long strides through the mud room,
headlong into the tool shed, wedges, winches, whetstones,
Henry and Denise onto the lawn tractor zigzag posthaste,
digging bars, mauls, chainsaws, crosscuts, six packs,
headlong onto the back lot, into the ancient libretto,
into the shadow, face-to-face with the stump from hell.

Henry hacks and strains with the crosscut,
sheds his sweater in the warmth of the day,
wipes the sweat and grime onto his tee shirt,
leans on the stump in the sun and sips his lager,
flexes his muscles lest they stiffen,
pounds wedge after wedge into the gnarl.

Together they warble the ancient libretto,
the songs of autumn's textures,
the songs of South Mountain:

> *A fine rich day on the back lot,*
> *a warm autumn morning to clear stumps*
> *and debris from the garden,*
> *to lay out winter legumes.*

Denise pokes her bony elbow into his side
as the fine rich day nears its end,
> *You'll split that stump right*
> *down the middle? Eh Henry?*

Perched on the stump to catch his breath,
Henry sips another October brew.
> *Next time more wedges and a bigger maul,*
> *for now let's call it a day.*

In the spring corn and scallions and snaps and squash
in the garden and a spray-painted sign on the stump,
> *Whoever shall pull the wedges out of this stump,*
> *be he a man or be she a woman, upon that person*
> *shall we confer a cord of gnarled firewood*
> *and a half-bushel of turnips.*

43

ABOUT THE AUTHOR

A 1967 graduate of Davidson College, noted author and poet George Miller first served his country as an officer in the U.S. Army during the Vietnam War. His subsequent civilian career saw him engaged with the Federal Deposit Insurance Corporation, the Lockheed Martin Corporation, and later as a successful CEO of his own computer software company. He is the author of numerous works, including *Wrap Your Ass in Fiberglass*, a novel, and *The Bucklodge Flagstop and Other Poems*. In 2019 he served as senior editor for *PAX: An Anthology of Southern Maryland Poetry*, incorporating the works of thirteen prominent regional poets of the lower Western Shore of Maryland.

CPSIA information can be obtained at www.ICGtesting.com
Printed in the USA
LVIW010329210920
666617LV00003B/34